# IT'S A
# CRISIS!
## NOW WHAT?

**The first step-by-step crisis communications handbook
for the global tourism and hospitality industry**

~

# "Every little thing counts in a crisis."

~ Jawaharlal Nehru,
Statesman of India

# IT'S A CRISIS!
# NOW WHAT?

The first step-by-step crisis communications handbook
for the global tourism and hospitality industry

Peggy R. Bendel

Sutherland House Publishing
Tucson, Arizona

"It's a Crisis! Now What?"
*The first step-by-step crisis communications handbook for the global tourism and hospitality industry*
by Peggy R. Bendel

Sutherland House Publishing
Post Office Box 8683
Tucson, AZ 85738
www.sutherlandhousepublishing.com

Printed in the United States of America

First edition 2012

ISBN-10: 1937614050
ISBN-13: 978-1-937614-05-8

# DEDICATED

*To everyone who has encountered
a crisis and lived to tell the tale –
and to the rest of you,
whose crises are in the future:
May they never arrive!*

# DISCLAIMER

This book is designed to provide information and ideas on crisis communications principles, tactics and practices. It is sold with the understanding that the publisher and author are not engaged in rendering legal or other expert assistance.

The purpose of this handbook is to educate readers on the principles and practices of crisis communications, with particular relevance to the global tourism and hospitality industry, and to complement, amplify and supplement other texts.

You are urged to read all the available material, learn as much as possible, and tailor the information to your individual needs. For more information, see the many resources in the Bibliography.

The author and Sutherland House Publishing shall have neither liability nor responsibility to any person or entity with respect to any loss or damage caused, or alleged to have been caused, directly or indirectly, by the information contained in this book.

If you do not wish to be bound by the above, you may return this book to the publisher for a full refund.

# ACKNOWLEDGEMENTS

The list is long, the appreciation heartfelt:

- My peer reviewers, colleagues and friends whose thoughtful comments and suggestions made this a much better book: Bill Baker, Sue Lomenzo, Hank Todd and Dann Lewis;

- Case study contributors Conceição Estudante, Lillibeth Bishop, Rob DeRocker, Malcolm Griffiths, Bob Schulman and Erica Pena-Vest (who filled in the story of the South Padre Island bridge); Linda Kundell and Anita Mendiratta, who are not in this volume, but have already contributed to the *next* book; and Norm Sklarewitz, who provided a journalist's perspective on the Costa Concordia sinking;

- The many colleagues, clients and friends who offered feedback and input on the cover, title, content and more: Karyl Leigh Barnes (kudos for finding some good quotations for me, too!), Don Bill, Mindy Bianca, Katia Carvalho, Miguel Carvalho, Dariel Curren, Yves Gentil, Ginny Gutierrez, Wendy Haase, Ken Hermer, Kristen Jarnagin, Kathleen Leuba, Andy Levine, Pat Levine, Ted Levine, Doug Mackenzie, Kay Maghan, Meredith Mirrington, Matt Owen, Katie Rackoff, Mary Rittman, Jean Walden, Scott West, and Jeanne Westphal;

- My nominee for "guru of all crises," Jim Lukaszewski;

- My editor Robin Quinn, whose keen eye and thorough link-checking saved many hours;

- Cover designer Jim Weems and interior designer Barb Weems, who made a "manuscript" into a "book";

- Mike Winder, whose illustrations relieve the monotony of text-text-text.

A special shout-out goes to former client and longtime friend Bill Baker, author of the seminal *Destination Branding for Small Cities*, now in its second edition. His invaluable encouragement and advice are the reason you're holding this book!

And last but far from least, to my family – husband Richard Gussaroff, daughter Margot Black and son-in-law Rob Aboulache, mother Dorothy Raftis and brother Jay Raftis and his wife Nancy – all of whom refrained from asking "How's your book coming?" until the very end!

~

"So when the crisis
is upon you, remember
that God, like a trainer of
wrestlers, has matched you
with a tough and stalwart
antagonist...that you
might prove a victor at
the Great Games."

~ Epictetus

~

"Character is not
made in a crisis;
it is only exhibited."

~ Robert Freeman,
English photographer and designer

# CONTENTS

~

"When things
are perfect, that's
when you need to
worry most."

~ Drew Barrymore,
American Actress/Director/Producer

## "Bad news always ripens badly."

~ James E. Lukaszewski, ABC, APR, Fellow PRSA
President, The Lukaszewski Group Division,
Risdall Public Relations – Crisis Communications Expert

# Why *This* Book?

*"The world has not just 'turned upside down.' It is turning in every which way at an accelerating pace."*

~ Tom Peters, business management author and speaker

Does that world need yet another book dealing with crisis communications, when there are many fine, well-researched volumes already in bookstores, classrooms and online?

You're holding the book I *didn't* find on the shelf or elsewhere, the one I wish I'd had at hand when, more than 20 years ago, I was first faced with advising a client or colleague in a quandary.

Outlining basic "rules of the road" and illustrated with examples drawn from the tourism and hospitality industry worldwide, this is a handbook, not a textbook or theoretical treatise, useful as those can be.

My objectives are simple:

- **Demystify the process** of creating the crisis communications plan you know you need, so you'll take the time to actually create it;

- **Bolster your confidence** in your own experience and abilities, and provide guidelines for drawing on them in a crisis;

- **Convince you to prepare *now*** for the inevitable crises you'll face (you'll sleep better at night, I can promise).

- **Help you protect and strengthen the brand equity and reputation** that your organization or destination has built up over the years.

Read and apply these principles, and you'll be ready to protect your destination or company and its reputation, and perhaps even save lives, by handling each crisis with calm, and aplomb.

Chapter 5 may be the most helpful aspect of this handbook is: a collection of "What would you do?" scenarios for you to brainstorm with your team.

The most important scenario of all is the last – yours.

Use your vivid imagination to detail your organization's worst-case nightmare, and think through NOW how you and your team would handle it.

Throughout this slim volume you'll find "Notes" pages: use them to jot down ideas that occur to you as you read each section, and to outline your response to each scenario.

Please let me know how your crisis communications experience evolves, and your thoughts on any part of the book, critical or not: your successful handling of a future crisis might even be featured as a case study in the next edition!

*Peggy*

Peggy@BendelCommunications.com

## "If things go wrong, don't go with them."

~ Roger Babson, American business theorist, author and founder of Babson College

# "When is a crisis reached? When questions arise that can't be answered."

~ Ryszard Kapuscinski,
Polish journalist

# CHAPTER 1

# Get Ready – There's a Crisis in Your Future!

*"Sooner or later comes a crisis in our affairs,*
*and how we meet it determines our future happiness*
*and success. Since the beginning of time every form*
*of life has been called upon to meet such crisis."*

~ Robert Collier, American Author

Have you experienced a crisis – or crises – in your career? Have you watched your peers succeed – or struggle – in overcoming a crisis of their own?

Whether or not there has been a crisis in your past, there's likely to be one in your future.

How effectively you communicate your company's or organization's position to the media and other publics may define the trajectory of your career – possibly even the fate of your destination, hotel, cruise line, airline or other entity. Most importantly, the health and safety of your staff, your customers, and even your community may be determined by your words and actions.

Let's take a closer look at a few crisis situations, some of which made headlines you may remember.

## What *IS* a Crisis?

You'll likely have no trouble recognizing a crisis when it hits! Do any of these seem possible?

- ► Food poisoning at your restaurant/hotel or on your cruise ship
- ► Guest's death on tour
- ► Terrorist attack
- ► Drowning in your hotel/resort pool
- ► Pandemic in your destination, in the countries your tours visit or the communities where your hotels are located
- ► Plane crash involving your clients, staff – or your airline
- ► Hurricane, floods or volcanic eruption disrupting air travel, tours and destinations
- ► Political unrest/regime change
- ► Unfavorable legislation
- ► Economic downturn/stock market crash
- ► Fire at your property or wildfires in the area
- ► Earthquakes, tornadoes, hurricanes
- ► Amusement park ride accidents
- ► Zoo/theme park animal incident
- ► Multiple crises at once (yes, it happens!)

A crisis is often said to represent *both danger and opportunity.*

Though that's perhaps not the "old Chinese proverb" it's reputed to be, I see the Chinese characters for "danger" and "opportunity" (below in that order) as beautiful graphic reminders of that concept:

Often the danger is readily apparent in a crisis. But how do you find *opportunity* in the face of a tragedy or natural disaster?

Your primary opportunity is often the chance to tell *your side* of the story, or how you successfully managed some aspect of a major crisis, mitigating or eliminating further stress for your customers, staff or the public.

That's an important perspective to keep front-of-mind as you undertake your crisis communications planning, and structure your key messages.

Here is just a small collection of crises I've been personally involved with:

► When *Hurricane Hugo* struck the U.S. Virgin Islands –
St. Thomas, St. John and St. Croix – on September 17,
1989, it was the first hurricane to make landfall there
in more than 50 years. Scouring St. Croix for nearly 24
hours, Hugo pulverized nearly every structure. From the
air, it appeared that someone had opened a box of pick-
up sticks and scattered them over the island, destroying
homes, businesses and, critically, hotels and resorts.

► *Reintroducing South Africa as a tourist destination* for
North American travelers, beginning in 1993, was an
intriguing challenge. This was a year before the election
of President Mandela, and there were fears that the
lead-up to that historic event would be bloody, due to
the tremendous amount of infighting between several
political factions. Fortunately, things remained relatively
calm, and the election was very well handled. However,
there were many months of anxiety and stress.

► My former firm was hired by the Oklahoma City
Chamber of Commerce 19 days before the *bombing of
the Alfred P. Murrah Federal Building* on April 19, 1995.
The case study on pages 64-66 tells the story of how
the people of Oklahoma City addressed and recovered
from the most deadly terrorist attack on U.S. soil prior
to September 11, 2001.

► *Hurricane Katrina* struck Baton Rouge, Louisiana, our
client at the time. That crisis is not yet over, as I write
this, almost seven years later – an example of how long
a crisis can actually last.

▶ The sister property of one of our hotel clients became the site of a *murder-suicide.* These things happen – no hotel can control what is happening behind a closed door. Unfortunately, the tragedy remained undiscovered for a week – imagine how unpleasant that situation was. They were fortunate that the story itself was engaging enough to the media that the critical question, "Why did no one enter that hotel room for a week?" was never asked.

▶ The *terrorist attacks of September 11, 2001* affected the entire world, not least during the three days immediately thereafter, when there were no flights. Many communities beyond New York City, Washington, D.C. and Pennsylvania were affected, and we'll review several on pages 54-56.

▶ The "AIG Effect"[1] caused widespread *criticism of meetings at resorts,* affecting hotels and resorts in Arizona, California, Florida, Las Vegas and beyond.

▶ *The economic downturn and uncertainty that began in 2008* is still affecting the whole world. It's more than three years later, and there's no resolution in clear view, resulting in a dramatic decline and slow recovery within the tourism industry, and many others as well.

---

[1] *The giant insurance company sought and received a $67 billion bailout from the U.S. government, yet held a lavish company retreat at an elegant resort shortly thereafter: both the bailout and the subsequent retreat received front-page coverage.*

- The first documented case of the *H1N1 virus* was identified in Texas. Eventually H1N1 appeared in practically every one of the 50 U.S. states, as well as many other countries, expanding internationally.

- The Hong Kong Tourism Board was a client when the *SARS virus* became a worldwide concern in 2003. More details on the case study can be found on pages 57-59.

- Anti-immigrant legislation, such as Arizona's SB1070 and similar bills in Alabama and several other states, led to *boycotts* of those destinations by associations, unions, meeting professionals and entertainers.

## How Do You Recognize a Crisis?

*"Don't look where you fall, but where you slipped."*

~ African proverb

There are many cogent definitions of "crisis" – at least one for every crisis communications book that has been published – such as:

- "A situation in which an individual or organization is faced with the prospect of fundamental change, usually sudden and unforeseen, which threatens to disrupt and overturn prevailing philosophies and practices." (**Tourism Crises: Causes, Consequences and Management**[2].)

---

[2, 3, 4] *See Bibliography for further details.*

► "An organizational crisis is a specific, *unexpected,* and *non-routine* event or series of events that create high levels of *uncertainty* and simultaneously present an organization with both *opportunities* for and *threats* to its *high-priority goals.*" (**Effective Crisis Communication: Moving from Crisis to Opportunity**[3])

► "A crisis is any situation that has a severe negative impact on a company's reputation and/or bottom line." (**The PR Crisis Bible**[4])

But the one I find most relevant to the global tourism industry is the simplest:

> *"A crisis is any situation that places lives, reputation or property at risk."*

# Case Study:
# Mudslides in Madeira

**Contributed by Conceição Estudante,** *Secretária Regional do Turismo e Transportes, Madeira, Portugal*

On February 20, 2010, the island of Madeira endured a drenching rain that caused flooding and mudslides, taking 42 lives and creating € 1.1 million in property losses – a catastrophic scenario whose images were transmitted to all the world.

From the first moment, the Regional Government, aware of this impact, assumed an attitude of great attention and responsibility in its communication with the media.

During the week that followed the disaster, we created a coordinated channel of information to reach all of our markets, and the Regional Secretary of Tourism and Transport gave twice-a-day press-briefings.

Simultaneously, in the Tourism Department, several actions were taken immediately to guarantee that:

► All visitors were located and safe.

► Any difficulties that affected tourists were identified and personal assistance given.

► All available means of communication, especially the Internet, were used to accurately transmit the limited extent of the impact, including the most important message that only a small part of the island was damaged and that neither the most important tourism areas nor any hotels were affected by the storm.

► After an urgent meeting, all private partners of the tourism sector – the hotels, tour operators, travel agencies, airline companies, the World Tourism Organization and the Portuguese diplomatic services abroad – were asked to use their own channels of communication to send the same messages about the situation and of the actions taken locally.

After the first week, when the commitment and assistance of all Madeireans had brought daily life nearly back to normal, we created a new promotional campaign, both for internal and external audiences. "Madeira, as beautiful as ever" was the concept used for foreign markets and "Este ano vou á Madeira" for Portugal, which incorporated the pro bono participation of Portuguese artists and opinion leaders.

During the following months, we organized numerous press and trade familiarization trips for operators and travel agents, culminating in November with hosting the annual Portuguese Travel Agency Association Congress. The Congress attracted more than 500 attendees, who were able to see our remarkable recovery for themselves.

*Conceição Maria de Sousa Nunes Almeida Estudante has served as Regional Minister, Culture, Tourism and Transports of the Regional Government of Madeira since June 2007. She was Regional Minister of Social Affairs from 2000 to 2007, and Regional Director of Tourism for Madeira from 1992 until 2000. Sra. Almeida has been an executive with Savoy and Santa Isabel Hotels, and has served on various tourism and airline task forces.*

# NOTES

_____

_____

_____

_____

_____

_____

_____

_____

_____

_____

_____

_____

_____

_____

_____

_____

_____

_____

_____

_____

_____

"Successful people
recognize crisis as
a time for change –
from lesser to greater,
smaller to bigger.

~ Edwin Louis Cole,
American author

# CHAPTER 2

# Four Essential Steps for Creating Your Crisis Communications Plan

*"The crisis you have to worry about most is the one you don't see coming."*

~ Mike Mansfield, American politician

By now I'm sure you can see how it's possible that a crisis *could* happen to your company or organization. So how do you prepare to communicate effectively, no matter what the crisis may be?

There are four simple – but essential – steps in creating a crisis plan:

**Step #1:** **Designate the key members of your Crisis Communications Team – and their back-ups.**

**Step #2:** **Brainstorm "what-ifs?" Be creative – and pessimistic!**

**Step #3:** **Determine who you will need to contact in various crises, and gather their contact details.**

**Step #4:** **Update Your Plan, FREQUENTLY!**

Let's look at each step in more detail…

# Step #1:
# Designate the key members of your Crisis Communications Team – and their back-ups.

There are four basic roles for your team, each of which may require more than one person, depending on the size and geographic reach of your company, as well as the extent of the crisis:

1. **Primary spokesperson:** normally your CEO, this person will make the initial statement on behalf of your company, but may need to step back from the spokesperson role in order to keep the company running;

2. **Secondary spokesperson:** a top executive, ideally introduced by the CEO as the day-to-day contact during the crisis.

3. **Technical experts:** depending on the crisis, this could be a health and safety officer, the CFO, CMO, CIO or others. Their role is to explain any necessary details about the specifics, but NOT to be the official spokesperson.

4. **Chief Communications or Public Relations officer:** rarely, if ever, seen on camera or in a spokesperson role, this person is the primary coordinator of the company's public response, advising the CEO and others on how best to express their position in a way that never obscures the truth, while assuring the company's point of view is clearly communicated.

Your CEO may be an excellent spokesperson: articulate, experienced, credible and unflappable with a camera in her face. But what if she's out of the country, on a plane, or among the dead or ill?

For your peace of mind, and your company's well-being, EVERY key member of your crisis communications team must have a back-up. When your COO (Chief Operating Officer) becomes the spokesperson in your CEO's absence, who steps into the day-to-day role of the COO? And if that person was already on the Crisis Communications Team in another role, who is *their* back-up when they become the spokesperson?

Every member of the team must have a back-up – or two – who are familiar with the responsibilities they might have to assume.

Our West-Coast Florida client knew that they were highly vulnerable to hurricanes. They had a comprehensive Crisis

Management Plan, as well as the Crisis Communications Plan that we had prepared for them. They knew that they would have a day or two notice of any hurricane, and wisely planned to have their major spokesperson flown to New York City. That way, we could make her available to the New York media. Excellent plan!

They eventually found themselves in the path of a hurricane about two years later. However, this time, that talented young woman was eight-and-a-half months pregnant, and unable to get on a plane. Fortunately, they had designated a back-up for her, and it was extremely helpful for us to have her back-up available.

## On-Camera Media Training: NOT Optional!

Your spokesperson and their back-up MUST have on-camera videotaped media coaching. Even if they have had it before they joined your organization, it's important for them to practice delivering a variety of key messages, prepared as 5- to 30-second sound bites, about your company or destination.

This doesn't have to be elaborate or expensive: a simple video camera, and a few hours, depending on the number of people in the session. You'll want to record two – ideally, three – "takes" for each person, with a brief, positive critique between each. And be sure the questions asked are tough, so they can practice delivering the three to five key messages of most importance to your organization in this crisis, no matter the question they are asked.

Having conducted media training for many clients, I've seen again and again how people react when the camera is turned on and they're in the proverbial "hot seat." They're likely to be a bit rattled at first, letting minutes go by before thinking to include their key messages (if they remember at all!). Invariably, however, on each successive take, they are more confident, and more adept at including the points they have practiced.

Remember, it's far better for them to be a little uncomfortable in front of *your* camera, than to be floundering for words in front of the media's.

Two or three 3-5 minute takes are usually sufficient, preceded by an hour or so of classroom training, including writing and practicing aloud a selection of key messages.

If you get a three- to five-minute in-studio interview – a long time for television – realize that just half of that time is yours for communication. The rest is occupied by the reporter introducing you, setting the scene, explaining the situation, and asking you questions.

In a crisis, your CEO may be interviewed by the media in the office, or at the chaotic scene of the crisis, not in the relative calm of the studio, adding the factor of unpredictability to the mix.

The outcome may not be a positive one, if your spokesperson isn't prepared with those key messages about your organization, your policies, or your perspective on the crisis in succinct sound bites.

Be prepared for resistance – everybody's reluctant to stand in front of that camera! If necessary, enlist the Chair of your Board of Directors to convince your CEO that they must be trained. Then have your CEO tell the Board Chair that *they* have to do it!

While they are likely to be the two people most in demand by the media, it's often valuable to include several other staff members; your brainstorming (that's the next step!) about potential crises will clarify which would be best.

**Learn from Travel Portland:** whenever a new Board Chair hasn't recently been through media training on their own, they must complete a session within the first month of their tenure. Bureau executives recognize that there's no predicting how soon their Board Chair will need to act as a spokesperson, and they want that person to be prepared.

# Step #2:
# Brainstorm "what-if's?"

Schedule a minimum of a half-day with your staff to explore all aspects of your product or services that might precipitate a crisis, including:

- ► The geographic areas in which you operate
- ► Political climate
- ► Security issues
- ► Financial concerns
- ► Complaints from staff or guests
- ► Weather
- ► Logistical issues (e.g. a tour operator might look at everything from their phone and Internet service to the airlines that carry their guests)
- ► Health considerations (food poisoning, epidemic, etc.)
- ► Employee satisfaction – or dissatisfaction.

You can undoubtedly add to this list; be sure to do so.

Consider including your Board of Directors and perhaps other stakeholders in the brainstorming session – especially if they might contribute experience or a perspective that would otherwise be missing.

Let your exploration be wide and deep; nothing's "too crazy" or "can't happen to us." It's helpful to ask everyone to share good – and bad – crisis experiences they've had, and to share what they learned from it.

Here are five essential questions to ask in your brainstorming:

1. What are the five worst crises that could befall our business or organization?

2. Which are the most likely to occur?

3. Which have the greatest potential to threaten our continued existence?

4. How would we deal with each?

5. How can we prepare NOW?

Remember that the Tragedy of 9/11 has been referred to as a "failure of imagination." At the time, no one in authority could conceive of such acts happening anywhere, let alone in Manhattan. However, in retrospect, the signs were there to be seen and acted upon.

# Step #3:
# Determine who you will need to contact in various crises, and gather their contact details.

Where do you find the people you need to find when you need to find them?

Crises rarely happen during business hours: nine to five, Monday through Friday. They happen on holiday weekends. They happen at two o'clock in the morning. They happen when your key people are halfway around the world.

Therefore, the most important element of any plan is *your contact list:*

▶ *Who* does *what?*

- ► *How* and *where* do I find them (even if the power is out, and it's Sunday on a holiday weekend)?

- ► This list needn't be 500 pages. The size will depend on the extent of the team you need to pull together, and the people and organizations you need to notify.

It's often helpful to establish a "telephone tree" for members of the crisis communications team, too, specifying who will call who, to inform and gather the team as swiftly as possible.

When you've developed your contact list, don't assume that you can rely on – or even access – data residing on your home or office computer.

What if the power is out? What if a tornado or a tsunami has destroyed your office and/or home?

Once we've prepared a Crisis Communications Plan for a client, it's emailed to every member of the team. A hard copy sits in a slim red binder on their desk, and they will also have a soft-bound copy at home, which accompanies them when they travel. (And I have copies of ALL of them, both digital and hard copy: on my computer, at home and when I'm traveling, too.)

On the following page – and available on my website (www.bendelcommunications.com/CrisisTools) for download as a Word document – is a sample Contact Information Sheet that we developed for the Massachusetts Office of Tourism. They're happy to have us share it, and for you to adapt it to your own needs. Add, but DON'T eliminate any of the fields already there!

**Date Completed:** _____

## (Name of Organization) Crisis Contact Data

Please be as complete as possible. Do **not** use PO BOX for address, and indicate suite, floor or apartment numbers. Thank you!

*All information will be kept confidential within the Crisis Communications Team.*

I am the (please check one) _____ Primary _____ Back-up contact for my organization.

Company: _____

Name/Title: _____

Office Street Address (Include Floor/Suite: No PO Box): _____

_____

City/State/Zip Code: _____

Home Address (No PO Box): _____

_____

Email: _____

Website: _____

(Area Code/Number for all below)
Office Phone/Extension: _____

Office Fax: _____

Home Phone: _____

Cell Phone: _____

Personal Email: _____

Emergency Contact: _____
(Name/Area code/Phone Number)

Website: _____

Twitter handle: _____

Facebook page: _____

ADDITIONAL: _____

Trust me, you may be glad to have that cell phone number for your Police Chief some day!

In the case of Hurricane Hugo, we knew it was going to come ashore on all three of the Virgin Islands (St. Croix, St. John and St. Thomas). However, it didn't appear to be as severe a storm as it was.

It was – of course – a Sunday night: the power and phones were shut down in anticipation, and for several days afterwards, the only operative phone line was to the Governor's office.

Wisely, his staff understood the critical importance of his personally updating the media, and gave us access to the Governor whenever we needed it.

# Step #4:
# Update Your Plan, FREQUENTLY!

Notice that the first field on that contact form is "Date Completed." There's nothing less useful than a database that's out of date; that's doubly true with your crisis contacts!

At least once a year, review your "what-ifs" scenarios. Many things may have changed. There may be new organizations or facilities in your community, or concerns that didn't exist last year. That means there may be new individuals you need to add to your Crisis Communications Contact Roster.

Be sure to reconsider the members of your core Crisis Communications Team at this point, too. People leave, move on to other jobs, new people are hired, and new skills are needed.

Perhaps there's an intern with a particular skill that would be useful – often, this is their facility and expertise with social media. During their internship, you may want to assign them to be a member of your communications team. They'll be supervised with someone with more seniority and perspective, of course. But it can be a great opportunity to tap into knowledge that might not have been available internally when you pulled your plan together.

On the other end of the spectrum, you might add a senior staffer with experience that could enhance your existing team, such as a crisis they have encountered and surmounted, or expertise in an operations area where a crisis could occur.

At least twice a year, update your contact list and distribute it to all team members. Put a reminder in your calendar for January and July – and don't "snooze" it for more than a day!

E-blast everyone on your list, attaching an editable copy of their latest form, and ask them to update it within a week. If they've moved, been promoted, taken another job or changed their home email-address in the past six months, they might not have thought to tell you.

You may find that someone is no longer appropriate as a contact because of they've been promoted or reassigned. If their organization is still important to you, ask for a replacement and contact that person directly to confirm their status and gather details.

# NOTES

_____

_____

_____

_____

_____

_____

_____

_____

_____

_____

_____

_____

_____

_____

_____

_____

_____

_____

"Real difficulties can
be overcome; it is only
the imaginary ones
that are unconquerable."

~ Theodore N. Vail,
American Industrialist

# CHAPTER 3

# Seven Keys to Success in Crisis Communications

*"In a crisis, don't hide behind anything or anybody. They're going to find you anyway."*

~ Paul Bryant, American college football coach

Good advice, Paul!

It may be tempting to head home – or to the nearest bar – when a crisis arises, but following the simple principles described here will be a wiser choice, and lead you toward a successful resolution.

Easy to remember, and an outline that can be adapted to any crisis situation, the seven keys include:

- ► Key #1: Don't panic!
- ► Key #2: Gather your team, launch your plan.
- ► Key #3: Know which crisis is yours.
- ► Key #4: Be proactive.
- ► Key #5: Make the power of the Internet and social media work for you.
- ► Key #6: Continually monitor media coverage.
- ► Key #7: Be consistent and transparent.

# 🔑 #1:
# Don't panic!

In dealing with any crisis, the most important mantra is *"Don't panic!"*

You may be *feeling* panicked. You may be thinking, *"How did this happen?! Could we have prepared for it? Will the company survive?"* But you're the very person who must never exhibit panic.

As the leader of a crisis communications team, the General Manager of a hotel, resort or conference center, or the CEO or COO of a cruise line, airline or other travel-related entity, you are the person your staff, your clients, your boss and certainly the media will look to as the primary source of information.

One of your most important roles is to reassure the people around you that you and your organization are prepared. They need confidence that you will handle the communications aspects of this crisis in a way designed to minimize its negative impact and maximize its positive opportunities.

It may help to remember this tongue-in-cheek comment:

*"Leadership has been defined as the ability*
*to hide your panic from others."*

~ Anonymous

If you've followed the preceding four steps in preparing your crisis communications plan, you'll be ready for the challenge!

# 🔑 #2:
# Gather your team,
# launch your plan.

*"When you face a crisis, you know
who your true friends are."*

~ Earvin "Magic" Johnson,
American professional basketball player

Whether you're connecting with your team members in person, online or a combination of both, NOW is the time you'll be grateful for the effort you took in compiling your contact list.

As renowned crisis communications guru Jim Lukaszewski recently told me:

"Most responses in crisis situations fail in the first hour or two. Management is unprepared for the two most challenging aspects of readiness for urgent situations: *the victim dimension* and *the strategy for first response* – literally, what you do first, second, third, etc.

"First, you stop the production of victims *(simply, those affected by the crisis)*. Next, you tend to the needs of victims. Third, employees and close constituencies need to be informed. Fourth, those indirectly involved or affected – government, neighbors, marketing partners – need to be brought into the information stream, and fifth, the self-appointed and the self-anointed, such as the various news and legacy media, are engaged.

"These actions should consume the first 60-120 minutes. Too often, problems become emergencies, crises or disasters due to the hesitation, timidity and confusion that occurs as the threatening nature of a situation rapidly unfolds, is recognized, and management is overwhelmed."

Your crisis communications role begins at the third point Jim outlines above; and you'll be prepared for all contingencies once you've mobilized your team.

You may find that, in the heat of the moment, someone who appeared utterly reliable seems unable to cope with the demands of the situation. That's one of the primary reasons you have a back-up for every member of your team. Call in the back-up to replace the original team member, or share the responsibilities. This isn't the time to criticize the individual, publicly or privately, no matter how frustrated you may feel. Let things cool, and, if necessary, deal with it when the crisis is over.

# ⚷ #3:
# Know which crisis is *yours*.

On September 11, 2001, and for many other crises as well, there would be multiple aspects of the same crisis. Most aspects of the crisis you face may not be under your control. If it is, for example, a natural disaster; and you're a hotel General Manager or Convention & Visitors Bureau (CVB) Executive, you probably won't go out and fight the wildfire, or hold back the floods. Someone else is taking care of that.

So what *is* your role in this crisis? Well, if you're part of a convention and visitors' bureau, you may need to contact the meeting planners you're working with keeping them posted if their meeting is coming up soon about what's going on and whether they may need to change their plans. If you're in city government, you may be interacting with the fire service, or – if the air quality is affected – with the health department.

On 9/11, my office was in midtown Manhattan. I was in Austin, Texas at the Texas Travel Industry Association's annual conference, and we also represented the State of Massachusetts, among other clients. That morning, I was on my way to the airport to begin our work developing a brand for Tacoma, Washington. In each of those places, there were very different aspects of the crisis.

In New York City, Washington, D.C. and Shanksville, Pennsylvania, there was a tremendous loss of life at the sites. Much of Manhattan was affected by disrupted communications and transportation, as well as potential health issues from the debris and smoke, combined with the shock and grief that persisted for some time.

In Texas, we faced a major marketing issue. I decided to stay in the State for the next several days, and with our client team and the advertising agency, we completely reworked the marketing plan for Texas tourism. Since potential visitors were very reluctant to get on planes and deal with dramatically increased airport security, there was no point in marketing to travelers in California and New York.

Instead, together we decided to intensify marketing within the State. They marketed South Texas to Northwest Texas and Central Texas to Northeast Texas. At the same time, they diversified their marketing with efforts to nearby states. In the next few months, for example, we brought Texas chefs to morning shows in Louisiana and Oklahoma to demonstrate their culinary prowess and entice viewers to drive "next door" to enjoy those dishes for themselves. This short-term activity aided the recovery for Texas, and set the stage for medium-and long-term success.

What was Boston's aspect of the September 11 crisis? Two of the planes departed from Boston's Logan Airport, so questions were directed at their Port Authority by the media and the general public. The questions ran along the lines of: *"What's going on with your security?" "How did those people get through security with box cutters?" "Is it safe to fly in and out of Boston?"*

In the Berkshires, a beautiful region of Western Massachusetts that offers an appealing combination of nature and culture, the crisis was of a more positive nature – although still a result of the tremendous tragedy. The region is very beautiful, very rural. There are many art museums, including one featuring the work of Norman Rockwell, as well as numerous beautiful walking-trails.

The weekend after September 11, many New Yorkers were eager to get out of town and reconnect with nature. It was a little too early for the fall foliage display, though it was starting, and harvest season was well underway. Within days, all accommodations were booked. There was no way to get a room, or a cabin. People drove to the Berkshires despite that, and then beyond to Vermont and other New England destinations, looking for a place to stay.

For hospitable hoteliers and innkeepers, their crisis was how to be as helpful as possible to the many people who they couldn't book – to help them seek out other places that had room and to help them make reservations at "the competition." Ultimately, their actions also enhanced the reputation of their own lodge or inn, and the community since they had been so helpful at such a difficult time.

## Case Study:
## The Hong Kong Tourism Board
## and the SARS Epidemic

**Contributed by Lillibeth Bishop,** *Hong Kong Tourism Board's Publicity and Promotions Manager for the Americas during the SARS crisis*

A decade before the Great Recession, there was a tourism "Perfect Storm." The body blows of September 11 and the Gulf War literally sucked the air out of international travel. Not long after the brief calm that followed these world-changing events, another mighty squall blew into Asia, then around the globe, in the form of an acronym – SARS (Severe Acute Respiratory Syndrome). While short as all acronyms are, the impact of the SARS pandemic was long and devastating.

The public was reading and watching the news streaming from Hong Kong, and it got worse as the Winter 2003 season peaked in January and early February. What was not seen nor heard was our unrelenting behind-the-scenes brainstorming and high-tech and high-touch outreach to the media, the travel trade, and the non-industry partners of the Hong Kong Tourism Board (HKTB).

To the credit of the Hong Kong Special Administrative Region government, its policy of total transparency during the SARS crises allowed HKTB to firmly position Hong Kong as a destination that cared deeply for the safety and health of its residents and visitors above all else.

Proactively engaging the media in a completely transparent manner, even at the height of the crisis, reinforced their trust in us, strengthened our credibility and earned us their admiration for our professionalism.

Though there was nothing we could do about the duration of the SARS crisis, the spread of the virus, or its containment, we knew that it would end, and so strategized relentlessly and created a communications plan. When the World Health Organization (WHO) and Centers for Disease Control and Prevention (CDC) finally lifted their respective travel advisory, we were ready to push the button. Around 2 AM, I got a call from Lily Shum, HKTB's Regional Director for the Americas. She was already in the office and I joined her a few minutes later. We immediately put into action our communications plan pre-designed for implementation at that very moment.

When news crews covered the first Cathay Pacific flight after the WHO and CDC lifted their travel advisory and passengers were interviewed, their coverage was smooth and seamless.

Fortuitously, we had invited journalist Peter Greenberg, then travel editor of the NBC *Today Show* and MSNBC, to broadcast his syndicated weekly radio show from Hong Kong that very weekend. His live reporting, including an on-the-street segment for MSNBC, revealed that residents, visitors and Peter himself could now enjoy Hong Kong without the masks that had become so familiar, and it was well-timed.

A media mega-familiarization trip, *Hong Kong Welcomes You,* drew almost a hundred top broadcast and print journalists from the United States, clearly demonstrating through their presence and subsequent stories how safe Hong Kong was. The sharp V-shaped rebound of arrivals from the U.S. into Hong Kong was the welcome result.

*Lillibeth Bishop was the Hong Kong Tourism Board's (HKTB) Publicity and Promotions Manager for the Americas during the SARS crisis. She is currently the Senior Director for Marketing and Public Relations for North America for Air China Limited, and the President/ CEO of Bishop International Group.*

# ⚷ #4:
# Be proactive.

*"Silence in crisis is a toxic strategy."*

~ James E. Lukaszewski, ABC, APR, Fellow PRSA
President, The Lukaszewski Group Division,
Risdall Public Relations – Crisis Communications Expert

A crisis may take place in your destination or on your property, or could be affecting the region where you're located. In any case, it's essential to be proactive in reaching out to the media, and your other publics (employees, partners, neighbors, clients and more).

The media have time and space to fill and they have to fill it on deadline, now often 24/7. Don't wait for the media to contact you. They need a source, and if you don't make yourself available, you may not like their choice. It could be a disgruntled former employee who has a grudge against you and who might reflect something that is inaccurate. It might be someone who simply doesn't know the facts, but has had a microphone stuck in their face; the human reaction is to comment, whether they're knowledgeable – or not.

If you're an appropriate source to comment in this crisis, be proactive. Issue a written factual statement (a simple press release or media alert will do it), and be sure to state the name and title of the spokesperson, so it's clear that person is an appropriate individual to contact. Also provide 24/7 contact information. I've seen many a website where, when you click on the "Media" or "Press" tab, there's a contact name, email and phone number – with a note that it's only active nine to five Monday through Friday.

*Always* provide a media contact who can be reached, even if it's an "info" number or email address that will be monitored by rotating staff members. A spokesperson *must* be available 24/7 or that vacuum is going to be filled by someone more accessible.

Consistency of messaging is essential to achieve credibility. The spokespersons must be updated regularly, and staff must know to refer all media queries to those individuals.

## Make Fact Sheets Available

Prepare for the eventuality of a crisis by creating simple fact sheets, backgrounders and talking points about your property, your destination, your airline, your attraction, your company. Industry-wide statistics are often available from national, state/provincial, regional or local tourism promotion organizations and industry associations, which can be used in the fact sheet and other materials.

Below is an example of such a document prepared a few years ago by Kristen Jarnagin, Vice President of Communications for the Arizona Lodging and Tourism Association. She compiled and distributed these talking points to media, legislators and officials throughout the State. During a period when there was disapproval of spending by companies that were receiving financial bailouts from the government, the AIG Effect referred to on page 25 led to cancellations of many corporate meetings throughout the country, hitting Arizona particularly hard. Having these statistics readily available meant that more people were using the information and it was right at their fingertips:

▶ *Business travel creates 2.4 million jobs. Meetings and events are directly responsible for 1 million American jobs.*

▶ *Business travel accounts for $240 billion in spending and $39 billion in tax revenue at the federal, state and local levels.*

▶ *The U.S. Travel Association estimates that 200,000 travel jobs were lost in 2008, and it expects another 247,000 to be lost in 2009.*

▶ *Each meeting and event traveler spends an average of $1,000 per trip.*

▶ *A new study shows that 87% of Americans who have attended an out-of-town meeting or convention for work say it's important to running a strong business.*

You can easily do something similar. There's always relevant information available from an industry organization, from your own research, from a university, from a national tourism body, or from the state tourism office. This information can help you speak authoritatively about the statistics that are particularly relevant to your situation. Have them at hand; and update them regularly – at least annually.

## NEVER! The Two Words Never to Speak

What are the two words you *NEVER* use when speaking with any media outlet, or to any audience, in a crisis? Which are the words that any listener, reader or viewer will interpret as "I did it," "Guilty!" or "It's our fault"?

You know what they are: *"No comment."*

Even if your legal counsel has told you that's all you can say, *NEVER* do so!

Be prepared with appropriate phrases such as: *"The situation is under investigation at the moment, so it would be premature to give you a statement. I'll be glad to do so, as soon as we know the facts."*

## Case Study:
## Terrorist Bombing of the Alfred P. Murrah Building, Oklahoma City

**Contributed by Rob DeRocker**, *Economic Development at Development Counsellors International (DCI) Marketing Consultant, and former Executive Vice President who directed the Oklahoma City assignment.*

The Oklahoma-City Chamber of Commerce couldn't have expressed our mandate more simply: *"Put us on the map."*

Hiring DCI on April 1, 1995, the Chamber recognized that Oklahoma City neither benefited from a good national profile nor suffered from a bad one. Instead, its image was negligible. This was keeping the City off the long lists, let alone the short lists, used by site-selection consultants looking for places for corporate expansions or relocations.

Nineteen days later, Oklahoma City was "on the map" – horrifically, due to Timothy McVeigh's bombing of the Murrah Building, which killed 169 people including 19 children under the age of six.

Within days, more than 2,000 media from all over the world were encamped in downtown Oklahoma City. Outlets such as *The New York Times* and ABC News created instant bureaus, churning out one dispatch after another in what had quickly become the most important story in the world.

As the communications team charged with telling the Oklahoma City "story," this presented us with a tantalizing dilemma. On the one hand, the City found itself hosting more international press at one time than it had in its collective history. But search and rescue operations were still taking place in the hope that people might be found alive in the rubble. It was hardly the time to pitch stories about Oklahoma City's plans for downtown revitalization.

So what to do? For the first couple of weeks, our counsel was for the Chamber to simply serve as a resource to the media on an as-needed basis. Chamber staffers set up a hospitality wing in the Medallion, then the city's lone downtown hotel, offering everything from coffee and donuts to area maps and advice on where the media could get haircuts.

And in time, the media relationships forged during that period allowed for the placement of stories that highlighted Oklahoma City's redevelopment plans and value proposition for expanding businesses.

Later that year, helped by the complimentary use of a Southwest Airlines jet, the Oklahoma Governor and the Mayor of Oklahoma City led a delegation on a "Thank You, America" tour, visiting the various communities that had sent rescue workers and thanking them personally for their help. Many stories that came out after the Oklahoma City Murrah Building bombing certainly exhibited what a warm and vibrant community Oklahoma City was, and what a tremendous "we shall overcome" spirit prevailed.

*Rob DeRocker is an economic development marketing consultant based in Tarrytown, NY and St. Croix, U.S. Virgin Islands. From 1990 to 2008 he was an executive with DCI and in 1996 was named principal and part-owner, working with some three dozen clients from the U.S. Virgin Islands to Anchorage, Alaska. Before joining DCI, he was speech writer for New York City's Deputy Mayor for Finance and Economic Development. He also served as Founding Executive Director of Habitat for Humanity in New York and recruited former President Jimmy Carter as a volunteer. He is often quoted in The Wall Street Journal, New York Times, CFO, Financial Times and many other business publications, and has appeared on CNN and Fox News, among other media.*

# 🔑 #5:
# Make the power of the Internet and social media work *for* you.

That we're living in the Era of the Internet is not news to any of us. Rather than dreading what can appear in comments on your own website, a Facebook page, YouTube, TripAdvisor or elsewhere, make that power work *for* you.

## South Padre Island:
## Smart Use of a Website in a Crisis

Here's just one example of doing this in a major crisis. South Padre Island, TX is connected to the mainland by a single bridge. On September 15, 2001 – just four days after 9/11 – at two o'clock in the morning, a steel-carrying barge struck one of the support piers, which caused two 80-foot sections of the bridge to drop into the water with a thunderous crash.

Fortunately, there was little traffic on it at that hour, but eight people were killed when their cars plunged into the water.

The South Padre Island Convention & Visitors Bureau had prepared a shadow page for their website (a simple page ready to be populated by factual content about severe weather or other issues), in recognition of their vulnerability as an offshore island to storms and other emergencies.

They promptly pulled down the entire visitor content on the site, knowing there was now no way for anyone to get to South Padre Island until ferry service was established. They immediately linked that shadow page to the State of Texas tourism website, which was also getting many inquiries from the media.

The Bureau updated the page frequently, beginning with briefings from the Mayor three or four times a day in the first few days, since it was a dynamic situation. The bridge was not back in service until late November, so updates on available ferry service continued for the duration. The visitor pages returned to the site within a week or so, once the ferry service was in place.

## Twitter as a Tool

Now we have Twitter, which has rapidly become an essential crisis communications tool.

My perspective on this changed during the H1N1 (aka "Swine flu") crisis, when the Center for Disease Control and Prevention (CDC) for the first time issued their updates through

Twitter, many times each day. Following them for our many clients who were affected by H1N1, it became clear how vital a tool Twitter was for receiving the most current details from an authoritative source such as the CDC.

The Federal Emergency Management Agency (FEMA), among others, now also uses Twitter extensively in such emergencies as hurricanes, wildfires and other natural disasters.

When you use Twitter in a crisis, you must tweet at least once a day. With just 140 characters available, a succinct update shouldn't take long. Often, limiting an important tweet to 120 characters is even more beneficial; this allows others a few characters to re-tweet it with a brief comment.

Including a link to more extensive details? Be sure to shorten it with bit.ly or another reliable link shortener, if not automatic on Twitter. Visit bitly.com, copy and paste the url into the form and click "Shorten," then use the brief link in tweet.

All tweets should be consistent with your overall messaging; and you'll want to decide who has authority to tweet for your organization, perhaps assigning one person to monitor and respond to all social media.

## Briefings and Visuals

When you're issuing a briefing statement, either in person, through PRNewswire, or another distribution route, always indicate the time and date of the current update and when you plan to issue the next update. And whenever possible, keep in mind the broadcast news cycle. Of course it's 24/7, but most stations will air scheduled newscasts in early morning, early and late evening, and perhaps at midday. If it's possible to schedule your briefing or distribute your update in time for them to cover it, you will win friends!

Broadcast and online media – print, too – also need visuals. While they will often prefer to use their own photographers or wire services for images of the crisis, they may welcome background images: maps of a community, layout of a hotel or resort, "before" shots of a town affected by a natural disaster. If you have those available, offer them.

The immediacy of video is a powerful tool. Be prepared with broadcast quality B-roll (unedited footage, with no sound or voiceover), as well as a hand-held video camera you can use to post up-to-the-minute videos and even interviews on your own website, your Facebook page, YouTube and other outlets.

Such videos should be edited only lightly, if at all. They can even be submitted – with full disclosure as to their source – to media outlets, and a link posted on relevant blogs and partner websites.

## Work Your Network

Most of us are on LinkedIn, Facebook or other social media networks. Often your Twitter feed will automatically show up there as well; however, if not, be sure to keep those networks informed, too. You'll find that people you would not normally think of updating about your situation also need to know – because they're being asked, or are simply involved in discussions about the crisis within the community or industry.

ALL of your staff – well beyond your executive team – must be updated, too. Your housekeepers and bellmen, your interns and junior salespeople go the grocery store, to church, to the gas station, meeting people who know where they work and who will ask them about the situation.

Be sure their information is accurate and up-to-date. "They never tell us anything" won't enhance your reputation – and you never know when a reporter is nearby! They must, however, always refer any direct media inquiries to the authorized spokespersons or you, as the crisis communications coordinator.

## The Power of One, Internet Style

This classic example of "the power of one" is an illustration of how powerful the Internet can be.

On March 31, 2008, Canadian musician Dave Carroll, with the band Sons of Maxwell, was traveling from Halifax, Nova Scotia to a gig in Nebraska, carrying his guitar onto the plane. While Carroll was changing flights at Chicago's O'Hare Airport, United Airlines gate-staff insisted that he check it. Despite his protests, they took possession of the guitar, then checked it in. As the musician waited for takeoff, a passenger behind him commented: "They're throwing around guitars out there!" You can imagine the outcome! When Carroll reclaimed it, the neck was broken, and the guitar was unplayable.

United Airlines denied any responsibility, saying it was his fault for not packing it properly. After receiving no satisfaction, as a musician, what was his recourse? After nine months in "a customer service maze," Carroll alerted the airline that he would be creating three songs about United, which he'd be posting on YouTube with the goal of getting 1 million viewers to watch them in the course of a year.

The first song, "United Breaks Guitars," was posted late in the evening of July 6, 2009; it had six hits before the musician went to bed that night. He woke to find the count had, encouragingly, risen to 300. Then an article in his hometown newspaper, posted on the paper's website, caught the attention of *The Los Angeles Times.* The paper wrote their own story for the Web, which went viral, leading to stories on CNN, *Late Night with David Letterman,* and beyond.

As I write this, the video of Dave's first song has been viewed ***11,888,250*** times, in countries across the globe (with over a million hits on the second one, and over 400,000 on the third). This led to a second career as a speaker for the talented and articulate Carroll. He has spoken before the U.S. Congress, presented at New York's Columbia Business School, and drawn attention to his 20 years of musical creativity. He has written a book, and now has a complaint resolution website!

If you haven't seen the videos yet, go to www.youtube.com, and search for United Breaks Guitars.

The enormous and unnecessary embarrassment it caused for United Airlines could have been avoided with a check for $1,200.

Instead, as reported in *London's Sunday Times* on July 23, 2009, when Carroll was told a final "No" by the now-infamous Ms. Irlweg:

*"Fine," he said to her, "But I'm going to write three songs about my experience with your airline, shoot videos for each of them, and then post them online." "Yeah, right," she must have been thinking.*

*But Carroll kept his promise. The first song,* United Breaks Guitars, *has now been played 3,515,357 times on YouTube, become a smash hit on iTunes, and has resulted in Carroll's rather bemused appearance on every major news network in America. Meanwhile, within four days of the song going*

*online, the gathering thunderclouds of bad PR caused United Airlines' stock price to suffer a mid-flight stall, and it plunged by 10 per cent, costing shareholders $180 million. Which, incidentally, would have bought Carroll more than 51,000 replacement guitars.*

*The airline's belated decision to donate $3,000 to the Thelonious Monk Institute of Jazz as a gesture of goodwill (Carroll said he was beyond the point of accepting money) did nothing to contain the damage.*

And how *did* United respond? Here's their rather stilted public statement:

*Dave Carroll's excellent video provides United with the unique learning opportunity that we would like to use for training purposes to ensure all customers receive better service from us.*

The final irony? Months later, heading to address a group of customer service representatives, Dave Carroll flew United – the first time since his guitar was damaged – to Denver.

They lost his bag.

# ⚷ #6:
# Continually monitor media coverage.

Monitoring media coverage is more of a challenge than ever. However, it's unquestionably even more essential as well.

While Google Alerts (and for measurement, Google Analytics) is a free and helpful tool, it doesn't cover everything. There are many monitoring services that can supplement that, by monitoring print, broadcast and online coverage for you – and they'll be the first to tell you that they normally only capture one-third of what's out there.

If you're involved in a major crisis with global impact or interest, you'll want to monitor the *national and international media* – BBC, Al Jazeera, Agence France Presse, CNN and others – that are pertinent for your situation.

Keep in mind that often *your local stations* are the source of feeds to national and international media, so don't overlook them, even if your crisis is a national story. Here's where long-standing relationships with your local media can pay off in a receptive ear when you are proposing they interview your spokesperson, representing your perspective on the issues.

## Beach Lovers in Boise?

A few years ago, beautiful Miami, Florida was in the news for an unsavory reason: several visitors had acquired hookworm, resulting from feral cats using the beach as a litter box. Precautions were clearly posted – primarily to wear shoes or sandals when walking on the beach. A semi-hysterical call to capture and euthanize the cats was recognized as a course of action that would attract far more negative publicity, and it was abandoned.

The initial coverage for the first week was strictly local. Within the week, however, a story was distributed on ABC News, filed as a health story rather than news. Monitoring showed pick-up in such markets as no-beaches Boise, Idaho – thousands of miles to the west and inland. Who would think that readers in Boise would be interested in a beach crisis in Miami? Thanks to the magic of monitoring, we could promptly update the story for them, noting that appropriate measures were taken and the beaches were safe.

## Monitoring Accuracy/Correcting Errors

You can't argue with a reporter or commentator's opinion, but you can refute their facts – if they are incorrect, or incomplete.

It's essential to have factual errors corrected promptly. As we all know, if a reporter is researching a topic, they'll often begin on the Internet. If the incorrect information is out there without any refutation, that is what's going to get used.

And it will be used again and again, because it's available there – forever! Recognize that when there's an anniversary – one year, two years, five years – there will be a range of opportunities to update the story, for the media and *for you.*

## Challenges in Monitoring

For many weeks leading up to the tenth anniversary of 9/11, the commemoration dominated almost all media in the United States. The tragedy itself, the rebuilding, the health of first responders, the economic consequences … there were many angles – all of which provided a chance for an expert in any of those fields, as well as those who were directly involved, to offer their perspective and their data.

To complicate the monitoring process even more, every media outlet from CNN on down is now encouraging each of us with a cell phone to be their eyes and ears. CNN calls this being an *iReporter*, and it involves emailing them images and video of a news story that might be of interest to its readers or viewers. It no longer requires a visit from a news crew sporting the logo of a major network to get you into the news. Very often, it's a resort guest, or even a staff member, who is being "the reporter;" and as smartphones become ever more sophisticated, this trend will continue.

## Virginia Tech Update

Many of you may remember the massacre of 32 people (students and teachers) at Virginia Tech in 2007. *USA Today* covered it extensively at the time. The University was in their literal backyard, as well as this being a national and international story. A serious issue during that crisis was that the shooter was roaming the campus for some time, not just a few minutes. The University was criticized for not having cell-phone numbers of their students, so they could text a mass message telling them to protect themselves. After the fact, they went a step further, and had a reverse 911 system put in place so they could call people. Those steps won't get coverage as they happen – the media has moved on – but an anniversary can present the opportunity to update information effectively, as Virginia Tech found in the following newspaper article.

This was, for Virginia Tech, an opportunity to get out that side of the story and to ensure people that they really had taken some very important steps thereafter.

## Va. Tech More Secure
## a Year after Massacre

BLACKSBURG, Va. – One year after a disturbed student killed 32 people and himself, Virginia Tech appears as tranquil as ever. A day before the anniversary of the massacre, students wearing their signature orange Hokie sweatshirts strolled on a rolling green quad.

## The Power of Images

This is an example of a story that ran in August 2010, on the fifth anniversary of Hurricane Katrina. The man in the image is holding a photograph of his former home, as he stands in the place where his residence used to be – now an empty lot. This is a dramatic illustration of the things that still needed to be done in the New Orleans area, and more powerful than many thousands of words.

## Facebook Can Help

Don't forget your Facebook page as a way to monitor external coverage. Often people will post a link to a story, or quote from one. Be sure you're posting, too, and responding to any posts that appear – to verify facts or correct misinformation.

## Case Study:
## Nancy Grace and the California
## Travel and Tourism Commission

**Contributed by Malcolm Griffiths,** *who heads the account team for the California Travel and Tourism Commission at Development Counsellors International*

March 11, 2011 is a date now etched into global history. A series of earthquakes measuring as high as 9.1 on the Richter scale rocked Japan. Tsunamis washed away entire coastal villages, buildings tumbled, and a meltdown ensued at Japan's Fukushima Dai-Ichi Nuclear Power Complex.

For our client, the California Travel and Tourism Commission, the greatest danger was a perception that California was affected by any of these unfortunate events – beyond the initial waves that damaged harbors from Seattle, Washington to Orange County, California. Most feared among the general public was the danger of radioactive particles blowing eastward to California, and across the U.S. While careful monitoring showed radiation levels were almost untraceable, posing no health risk, the situation created near-hysteria amongst the U.S. media.

Contributing to the craziness was Nancy Grace, popular host of *HLN* (*Headline News,* a division of CNN). She proclaimed that California was in a state of emergency, owing to the radiation threat on Monday, March 21 – though disputed on air by her guest, Accuweather meteorologist Bernie Rayno.

An inflammatory comment from such an influential media representative could be detrimental to California's $29.9 billion tourism industry. When we were alerted, our team at Development Counsellors International immediately drafted an email to Ms. Grace's entire production team (to be sure *all* producers were aware). In the email, we asked that she correct the remark, and included links to statements from the California Governor's Office, the California Department of Public Health, and the California Emergency Management Agency.

Within minutes of receiving the email, Grace cleared up the confusion on air, and one of her producers called our office to confirm. Comedy Central's *Daily Show* later that same night covered the incorrect re-mark, and her swift rescind.

Here's the email we sent:

**Sent:** *Tuesday, March 22, 2011 8:25 PM*

**Subject:** *Please Correct 3/21 Comment by Ms. Grace: California Has NOT Declared a State of Emergency re Radiation Threat*

**Importance:** *High*

*Our media monitoring activities on behalf of our client, the California Travel and Tourism Commission, indicated that Nancy Grace commented last night, in an exchange with weatherman Bernie Rayno, that California had declared a state of emergency due to the threat of radiation reaching the state as a result of the damage to the Fukushima Nuclear Plant.*

*I'm pleased to say that California has not declared such a state of emergency. While radiation is being monitored throughout the region, there is no expectation that any significant radiation has reached, or will reach, California or any part of the West Coast of North America.*

*We know you are eager to present only accurate information to your viewers. And since Ms. Grace is highly regarded as a respected authority by her many dedicated fans, we would greatly appreciate it if she could briefly correct the information provided on her show last evening.*

*Please see the statements last week from:*

- *Governor Brown http://gov.ca.gov/news.php?id=16940*

- *The California Department of Public Health (CDPH) http://bit.ly/hRN8DB*

- *California Emergency Management Agency (Note there have been no statements released since 3/15, since the danger has passed.)*

*If we can be of further help, please call my colleague (Name) at (Cell phone #).*

*Many thanks,*

*Malcolm Griffiths*

*Malcolm Griffiths is a Vice President in the Tourism Practice of Development Counsellors International (DCI), a New York City-based destination marketing firm. He has overseen the public relations and marketing campaigns of some of the world's most renowned travel destinations including California, Greater Miami and the Beaches, and Tasmania. Prior to joining DCI, he was an integral member of Tourism Australia's North America communications team in Los Angeles.*

# ⌐ #7:
# Be consistent – and transparent.

*"I am a firm believer in the people. If given the truth, they can be depended upon to meet any national crisis. The great point is to bring them the real facts."*

~ Abraham Lincoln, 16th President of the United States

Consistency and transparency help establish credibility. Sticking to the facts, without speculation on what might – or might not – be involved in creating, prolonging or mitigating the crisis at hand is the foundation of all communications.

Three simple tactics help:

- Use the same spokesperson, if possible.

- Hold briefings/issue statements on a schedule (daily, AM/PM, hourly).

- Release information to *all* media simultaneously.

If your crisis is 24/7, it can be difficult to obey the first principle of using the same spokesperson. But if someone has established a good rapport and trust with the media, and if there will be frequent briefings, it's best to stick with the same source.

It's essential to carefully observe how the relationship is working, however. Occasionally, the initial "good guy" can slip, taking your organization's reputation along for the ride.

## Wrong Spokesperson/Wrong Words

You may have seen the extensive broadcast coverage of the 2010 BP oil platform explosion and consequent oil spill in the Gulf of Mexico, affecting the Louisiana, Mississippi, Alabama and Florida coastal resort areas as well as their fishing industries.

The original spokesperson was BP's then-CEO Tony Hayward, who was initially praised. He didn't appear in a suit and a tie as though he had just walked out of an office. His sleeves were rolled up and his tie had been loosened, if he had been wearing one at all; he looked like he was out there in the trenches with the workers conducting the clean-up.

But soon his words and behavior were highly criticized. You may remember his spontaneous and unconsidered comment, undoubtedly heartfelt: "I want my life back." Assuredly, so would the 11 men who were killed on that oil rig that exploded. To then be seen relaxing at a yacht race – albeit with his family – while the crisis was still ongoing was, to say the least, unwise.

Those two errors alone might have cost him his job… and they certainly led to some "collections" of Tony Hayward's gaffes, before and after the spill, such as: *http://cnnmon.ie/cYlHc9* and *http://www.bbc.co.uk/news/10360084.*

This raises the obvious question: Since he was known for verbal "slippage," why did his Board not demand he be media-trained?

## On Being Impartial

If your crisis makes it essential to issue frequent briefings, do them on a schedule. Whether they're hourly, morning or evening, once a day, do not offer an exclusive to any media – even if one of them initially alerted you to the crisis. Instead, release news to all of them simultaneously. Any media outlet – or reporter – that has been scooped will remember that forever. Reporters move from community to community – making a friend in the media can be invaluable, and one of the ways to do it is to be impartial about the way you distribute your briefings and updates.

## Case Study:
## Frontier Airlines Hijacking

### Contributed by Bob Schulman,
*founder of WatchBoom.com*

I was the director of PR for the original Frontier Airlines, when one of its planes was hijacked in Nebraska by an armed man. Somehow he got through the airport security checkpoint and forced his way on the aircraft, as it was getting ready to pull away from the gate. The cockpit door hadn't yet been closed, and the hijacker pointed his gun at the pilot, demanding to be flown to Atlanta.

A mob of local and national media quickly showed up at company headquarters in Denver. Following our crisis plan, we had employees stationed at the reception desk to badge the reporters (required of all visitors) and escort them to a nearby meeting room designated as the press room for emergencies. There, between frequent briefings, airline officials were available to the media for one-on-one interviews. At the same time, other employees escorted TV crews out to the airport runways to get "B roll" footage of planes landing and taking off.

Our willingness to work with the media gained their trust, which paid off at the end of the incident after our jet landed in Atlanta. There, a local radio station was reporting that the hijacker had killed several passengers.

We asked the media in our briefing room to withhold such reports until we could confirm the shooting one way or the other. They agreed.

A few minutes later, we were able to confirm that the hijacker had shot and killed himself, but harmed no one else. Had the earlier report gone out, it would have created panic among the families of all the passengers on the plane. It may have even prompted police to storm the aircraft.

*Bob Schulman spent four decades as a public relations executive for six airlines and handled "more crises than I'd like to remember, from hijackings to wheels-up landings to boardroom shake-ups." He was a co-founder and vice president-corporate communications for Denver-based Frontier Airlines, from which he retired to begin a second career as a freelance travel writer. His articles appear in more than two dozen magazines, newspapers and websites. Schulman is also co-owner and travel editor of WatchBoom.com, a monthly online magazine for baby boomers launched in 2009. He is a member of the Society of American Travel Writers and the Mexico Writers Alliance.*

# NOTES

# NOTES

# "Crises refine life. In them you discover what you are."

~ Allan K. Chalmers,
Scottish writer

# CHAPTER 4

# Crisis Over!
# (But you're not done yet...)

*"This, too, shall pass."*

~ William Shakespeare

At last, the crisis is over – after a couple of days or weeks or months. What do you do now?

- ► Breathe a deep sigh of relief.
- ► Congratulate your team on doing such a good job and putting in those extra hours.
- ► Go home and get some sleep!

And then, pull out that Crisis Communications Plan for a critical look at what needs to be updated.

- ► Did you know how to reach everybody?
- ► Are there steps that you could/should have taken, or contacts you should have had in your database?
- ► What else will you need to know/to do the *next* time?

## Before the *Next* One

Here are a few issues to consider…

### 1. In-house PR team, or outside firm?

When you're facing a crisis, is it better to be communicating through an in-house team, or through an experienced PR firm?

The ideal, of course, is to have both.

An in-house team knows the landscape, knows the players as an outside firm rarely will. However, an experienced PR firm is more likely to have a broad crisis background and a more extensive network of media contacts – that is their bread and butter.

If you don't have a PR firm on retainer, sometimes it's possible to arrange to have a suitable company or individual "on call." This could be a local agency, or, if you're vulnerable to hurricanes, tornadoes, or other natural disasters, a firm outside the area that could be affected. In the second case, the firm might charge a small monthly fee to be available to you as needed, then a daily or hourly rate during a crisis.

Interview several firms, to determine which is an appropriate match for you, and is willing to work on the basis you need. Your goal is to find a firm who is knowledgeable about your issues, and that you can call in the middle of the night, during a weekend, on a holiday – whenever that next crisis occurs.

Outside counsel will never be your spokespersons, of course: but it is helpful to have them contributing their expertise and guiding the process as part of your team.

**2. Keep communicating with your key audiences, even when there's *not* a crisis.**

Ongoing communication is an important element in developing trust.

At a recent crisis-communications seminar I conducted, an attendee said their organization was facing what should have been a minor issue, due to dropping one element of their program of public activities.

Unfortunately, their Executive Director didn't want to discuss it publicly; he just didn't like to deal with anything that might be negative. The program had continued for some years. The cessation of it was known to some of the staff and customers, and this had already caused some hard feelings. It was going to be missed by many devotees, when the facility opened again for the season.

And so, why not tell people? Why let there be rumors out in the community about it, when an explanation of the budgetary constraints would be unwelcome, but understandable. You want to control that message and you can only do so by communicating.

This story illustrates just a few reasons why you should be communicating on a regular basis, and the point that the audiences you would be communicating with will be both external and internal.

## The Universal Question: "What's in it for me?"

Always keep in mind your audience's prism: *"What does this mean to me?"*

Whether a meeting planner, a journalist, a consumer or a politician, each needs to know how your news will impact them. For the journalist, *"Is it a good story?"* For the meeting planner, *"Is that hotel going to be closed for six months? Do I have to move my meeting?"* For a traveler, *"I was going to take my vacation there. Should I go someplace else?"*

## 3. Leverage the power of many.

You have many potential partners in this industry. Be sure to communicate with your legislators; very few of them come from within the tourism industry, and therefore they do not always understand what an economic driver and job creator tourism is. Educate them *before* a crisis occurs. You may create strong supporters, and avoid the possibility of legislation that would negatively affect the industry.

The general public also lacks an appreciation of the economic aspects of tourism, as well as the benefits – both economic and social – that tourism brings to their community. It's important to demonstrate how tourism relates to the personal interests of residents, and provides specific benefits. For instance, golfers might have fewer courses to play on; art-lovers, fewer museums and galleries; gourmands and gourmets, fewer restaurants.

## 4. Repetition of your key messages to your varied audiences is essential.

Your key message might be the number of jobs that are supported by the industry, the economic dividends, the impact on your local tax bill as a resident, etc. Be sure that your industry partners – local, regional, national and international – know what's happening.

Mobilize supporters from within and outside the industry, throughout your community. Don't overlook community groups, service clubs, schools and colleges, chambers of commerce – all are often eager for relevant speakers to address their members. And, of course, your local media are a prime audience.

# NOTES

_____

_____

_____

_____

_____

_____

_____

_____

_____

_____

_____

_____

_____

_____

_____

_____

# NOTES

_____

_____

_____

_____

_____

_____

_____

_____

_____

_____

_____

_____

_____

_____

_____

_____

_____

_____

# "Close scrutiny will show that most 'crisis situations' are opportunities to either advance, or stay where you are."

~ Maxwell Maltz,
surgeon and author

CHAPTER 5

# What Would *YOU* Do?
# Scenarios for You to Analyze

*"There cannot be a crisis today;
my schedule is already full."*

~ Henry Kissinger,
American political scientist

Since our schedules are *always* full, though perhaps not as full as Mr. Kissinger's, get some practice **now**!

I encourage you to use the following scenarios in your brainstorming, or to create others that are more relevant to you. In either case, work your way through them with your Crisis Communications Team once or twice a year. Situations change. It's always good to have that experience thinking on your feet.

The scenarios that you explore may not be ones that you actually have to contend with. However, just the fact that you're thinking along those lines can be very, very helpful.

## Embezzling from the Museum

You're the Assistant Director of a small, but growing museum. It's Friday night, and you're heading home after drafting the invitation to the museum's first major exhibit, which will firmly establish its reputation regionally and nationally. The Director calls you into her office, appearing upset. As you sit down, she hands you her resignation and says, "By tomorrow, you'll be heading up this place."

You scan the document. She is acknowledging embezzling more than $250,000 from the Museum, to cover her husband's gambling debts. The annual audit has uncovered the loss, and it will be public knowledge within hours.

The upcoming exhibit is now in jeopardy. The prized collection is on loan from a personal contact of hers, an outstanding collector known for his rigorous moral code. He is likely to be reluctant to be tainted by the scandal.

Your BlackBerry buzzes. It's the local newspaper, and you send it to voicemail. The call is from a reporter who has already done several stories about the exhibit. He's heard about the missing money, and plans to break the story in the morning – he would welcome a quote from you.

- What do you do?
- Who do you call first?
- What are the potential consequences?
- Can you turn this into a positive experience for the museum?

# NOTES

## Sliding into Tragedy

It's July, peak season for your resort, which combines some of the best dining in the area with a good 18-hole golf course and a marvelous pool and water slide. The place is ideal for families, who can enjoy a few days at bargain rates before the kids head back to school.

As the General Manager, you're meeting with your Director of Sales to plan some holiday activities. A call comes in from the front desk.

There's a news crew there, and they've heard there has been a drowning at the pool. A child, who came down the waterslide too quickly, hit her head on a protruding rock, one of many positioned there to make the setting seem more natural. The news crew had been alerted by another guest, who sent an image of the scene on their smartphone to the news desk. Your security staff has prevented the news crew from going beyond the front desk, but they're getting impatient and grumpy.

Immediately, you contact the Pool Manager. She confirms the sad facts, and says she's just completed trying CPR on the child without success. The Pool Manager didn't call you, because she felt it was most important to try to save the child's life.

- Now what?
- Do you go to the pool, or the Front Desk?
- What do you say to guests at the pool, who have watched this tragedy unfold?
- How do you address the issue with other guests?
- Guests arriving in the next few days?
- What do you say to the news crew?

# NOTES

_____

_____

_____

_____

_____

_____

_____

_____

_____

_____

_____

_____

_____

_____

_____

_____

_____

## Wildfires and Athletes – Not a Good Mix

As the Marketing/Sales/PR Director of a medium-sized Convention and Visitors Bureau, you're anticipating the arrival of the biggest piece of business you've ever booked: 750+ participants (players, parents, coaches and supporters) in a State middle-school softball tournament that's taking place in your town this weekend. It's the first time the town has hosted an amateur sports event of this caliber, and could mean great things for future business – if all goes well.

Three days ago, a wildfire broke out about 10 miles away in a remote area, where it had time to build before being spotted. Strong winds and continued warm, dry weather are predicted for this weekend, increasing the possibility that the fire may spread out of control of the firefighters who have been battling the tough blaze since it was discovered. Rural homes are now threatened, and the fire is moving your way. The travel planner for the teams coming to the tournament is calling to see what you recommend. What do you advise, with only two days until they arrive?

And of course, the local media is covering both stories – the fire *and* the tournament.

• What will you say to the travel planner and the media?

# NOTES

## Tour Operator's Nightmare Comes True

You're ready to leave for the weekend, after one of the busiest weeks ever at Anonymous Tours. You've booked more business than ever in one week of the firm's history, all tours for the next six months are full, and you're looking forward to a relaxing weekend, starting with a celebratory dinner with a dear friend, in an hour.

The phone rings, as your hand is on the door. As the answering system takes the message, you quickly recognize the voice of one of your best and most loyal clients, though she is nearly hysterical.

You immediately intercept the call, realizing that just six days ago, she and her husband departed on your "African River Adventure" tour, the dream of a lifetime for them. Between her sobs, she tells you he became ill two days ago, and your tour guide assured her it was just the typical gastric problems common to Africa travelers. But he worsened yesterday, and this morning, she woke to find him unresponsive. He died within hours.

The tour guide was clearly upset, but left to accompany the rest of the group on the day's land tours. He promised to notify authorities and arrange for the body to be returned home, but he sent the group back without him. He has not returned to the ship, which is now about to sail for the next port, and your client is frantic. What should she do? Who should she call? How does she bring her husband home?

And since she believes that the tour guide did not get her husband the care he needed, she's planning to sue your company, the tour guide, and anyone else she can.

- How do you respond to her?
- Who do you call next?
- Is your company in jeopardy?

# NOTES

## Cruise Ship on the Rocks – The Company, Too?

During the private cocktail party for repeat guests during a lengthy cruise in the Far East, hosted by the ship's Captain, an ominous sound is heard, as the whole ship – carrying more than a thousand guests – shudders to a stop.

As the ship begins to list slightly, the Captain tries to reassure these most important guests that all's well. Then a member of the crew suddenly rushes to his side, and his face pales.

With assurances that the ship has simply run aground on an uncharted sand bar and will soon free herself, the Captain departs for the bridge. He asks everyone in the room to remain calm, and in the room, to which he promises to return swiftly.

As the new PR and marketing representative for the cruise line, you're escorting a group of trade media and luxury market travel agents. Most of them have joined the cocktail party as honored guests, but you suddenly realize about two dozen are not in attendance.

The lights in the room flicker and dim, quickly replaced by emergency lighting; guests are chatting nervously, eager to return to their cabins. You begin to gather your group, and a quick head count shows some have already left the room.

Another lurch, and screams echo throughout the ship, as the list increases a few degrees, making walking – or even standing – difficult.

Your group looks at you expectantly for direction, as the recent tragedy of the Costa Concordia, costing 34 lives and a $45 million ship, flashes through your mind.

- What do you advise them to do?
- Should you search for the Captain or another crew member, all of whom have vanished from the reception, except for the wait staff, who speak little English?
- How much worse could the situation become, and what are your priorities?

# NOTES

## A Mighty Wind Wreaks Havoc

A powerful wind-and-rain storm surprises London and its suburbs, where your offices are located, on a Sunday night, with record-breaking winds, which smash windows throughout the office building, knocking out all power: phones, computer and lighting.

Worse yet, some of those windows were in your offices, with the accompanying rain drenching desks, phones and computers.

After an inspection by the local Office of Public Safety, the building is declared unsafe for the foreseeable future. All occupants are prohibited from entering, as the staff discovers when they arrive for work on Monday morning.

More than 150 of your clients are on a variety of tours around the world, several in areas which have been in the news this weekend:

- Egypt, where unrest seems to be breaking out yet again;
- Greece, where uncertainty is rampant, and demonstrations have spread beyond Athens to the usually tranquil islands;
- Thailand and Myanmar, where the results of the recent elections have angered some of the opposition, which is threatening to kidnap tourists.

You need to notify many people about your situation, with no idea when you will be able to reoccupy your offices, or whether or not your data is intact.

- What do you do first?
- And next?

# NOTES

# Reward! Lost (Champion) Dog

The Westminster Kennel Club Dog Show concluded yesterday in New York, and the airline for which you are handling public relations will be shipping several hundred of the dogs around the country.

A text message buzzes: your client asks you to call her immediately. She tells you the airline's station manager reports that the lock on a kennel opened on the tarmac and one of the dogs – a Best of Breed winner, and contender for Best in Show – escaped. The owner and handler, both of whom had boarded the flight, have disembarked and are distressed and furious, loudly blaming the airline for carelessness with their precious cargo, more valuable than ever after her win. The handler, who was responsible for securing the kennel and who recently had a heart attack, is having chest pain.

The dog is nowhere to be found: terrified, she seems to have run away from the baggage handlers, possibly toward a nearby highway. The story is already spreading via Twitter and Facebook, accompanied by images of the empty crate taken by passengers who saw the incident as the plane was being loaded.

The Show is a major piece of business for the airline, a sponsor for several years, running TV ads proclaiming their "special care" for their four-footed passengers.

In a similar incident several years earlier, the airline involved (not your client) was harshly criticized on social media, and saw its reputation and its bookings plummet. The dog's body was found several weeks later, apparently having been struck by a car; the discovery started the controversy yet again, with animal advocate websites, bloggers and social media users outraged. Your client is anxious that a similar outcome could affect them, escalated by the dog's many fans, and exacerbated by her value.

The media have been calling and images are on the noon newscast, with further coverage expected at 5. The social media conversation is heating up, with many people now complaining about their own experiences on the airline, and a petition is circulating whose signers vow to boycott the airline until the situation is resolved.

What do you recommend she do in addressing the mainstream and social media? If the dog is found dead – or never found – how should she handle the news?

# NOTES

## My Worst-Case Scenario

_____

_____

_____

_____

_____

_____

_____

_____

_____

_____

_____

_____

_____

_____

_____

_____

## How I Will Resolve It

_____

_____

_____

_____

_____

_____

_____

_____

_____

_____

_____

_____

_____

_____

_____

_____

"Faced with crisis,
the man of character
falls back on himself.
He imposes his own
stamp of action, takes
responsibility for it, and
makes it his own."

~ Charles de Gaulle,
French general, writer and politician

# BIBLIOGRAPHY

Adubato, Steve, Ph.D. *What Were They Thinking? Crisis Communication – The Good, the Bad and the Totally Clueless,* Piscataway, NJ: Rutgers University Press, 2008.

Anthonissen, Peter F., ed. *Crisis Communications*. London and Philadelphia: Kogan Page Ltd., 2008.

Bryson, Bill. *A Short History of Nearly Everything*. Broadway Books, 2003.

Cohn, Robin. *The PR Crisis Bible,* New York, NY: Robin Cohn, 2007.

Coombs, W. Timothy. *Ongoing Crisis Communication: Planning, Managing and Responding,* 3rd ed. Los Angeles: SAGE Publications, 2012.

Dezenhall, Eric and John Weber. *Damage Control: Why Everything You Know About Crisis Management Is Wrong*. New York and London: Penguin Group, 2007.

Fearn-Banks, Kathleen. *Crisis Communications: A Casebook Approach,* 4th ed. New York and London: Routledge, 2010.

Fink, Steven. *Crisis Management: Planning for the Inevitable*. New York: AMACOM, 1986.

*Harvard Business Review on Crisis Management,* Boston: Harvard Business School Publishing, 2000.

Henderson, Joan C. *Tourism Crises: Causes, Consequences & Management,* Burlington, MA: Butterworth-Heineman, 2007

Lukaszewki, James, *Why Should the Boss Listen to You? The Seven Disciplines of the Trusted Strategic Advisor*, San Francisco: Jossey-Bass, 2008

Lukaszewki, James, *Lukaszewski on Crisis Management*, Danbury, CT: Rothstein Books, September 2012 (Jim has many other useful books and articles available through his websites www.e911.com and www.risdallpublicrelations.com)

*Now Panic and Freak Out,* Summersdale Publishers Ltd., Chichester, UK, 2010.

Ulmer, Robert R., Timothy L. Sellnow, and Matthew W. Seeger. *Effective Crisis Communication: Moving from Crisis to Opportunity,* 2nd ed. Los Angeles: SAGE Publications, 2011.

# LIST OF CASE STUDIES

"In the best of times, our days are numbered anyway. So it would be a crime against nature for any generation to take the world crisis so solemnly, that it put off enjoying those things for which we were designed in the first place: the opportunity to do good work, to enjoy friends, to fall in love, to hit a ball, and to bounce a baby."

~ Alistair Cooke,
American journalist and commentator

# ABOUT THE AUTHOR

Peggy Bendel is a globally recognized expert in travel marketing, crisis communications and media training. She has worked for destination and hospitality clients around the world, from Australia to Arizona, California to Chile, South Africa to Sweden.

A principal in the seminal *I Love New York* campaign, Peggy began her career as a travel writer for the State of New York. She has worked in the areas of economic development and international trade, as well as tourism.

Peggy joined Development Counsellors International (DCI), the leader in marketing places, in 1985 to re-launch their tourism division, and lead the public relations campaign for the Australian Tourist Commission's (now Tourism Australia) iconic "Shrimp on the Barbie" campaign.

She launched Bendel Communications International in 2009, and now represents a variety of destinations, tour operators and hotels, as well as continuing to work with DCI. She conducts marketing, crisis communications and public relations workshops and boot camps in the U.S. and around the globe.

Recognized with a "Lifetime Achievement" award by the Hospitality Sales and Marketing Association International, Peggy is a frequent speaker at conferences and workshops around the world. She contributes to a range of industry publications, including *Travel Marketing Decisions, PR Tactics* and *O'Dwyer's PR Report*, and has been profiled in a variety of international media, most recently in Austria, Canada and Portugal.

She sits on the Boards of the Association of Travel Marketing Executives (ATME.org), the Public Relations Society of America's (PRSA.org) Travel & Tourism section, and the Ecology Project International (EcologyProject.org). She has recently been nominated to the Board of the Destination and Travel Foundation, and is a member of the Society of American Travel Writers (SATW.org), the International Ecotourism Society (Ecotourism.org), the American Indian Alaska Native Tourism Association (AIANTA.org) and other industry organizations.

A frequent speaker at conferences around the U.S. and internationally on the topics of branding, crisis communications, marketing, public relations and social media, Peggy is also an experienced media coach and presentation trainer.

A graduate of Georgian Court College (now University), Peggy was named to their centennial "Court of Honor" in 2008. She also studied at NYU's Graduate School of Public Administration.

Peggy lives in New York and Tucson, AZ, with her husband Richard Gussaroff and multiple felines.

**You can reach Peggy via email at:**
**peggy@bendelcommunications.com**

**Visit her website at:**
**http://www.bendelcommunications.com/**

Sutherland House Publishing
Tucson, AZ 85738
SutherlandHousePublishing.com

# QUICK ORDER FORM

**Web orders to:** www.sutherlandhousepublishing.com

**Email orders to:** orders@sutherlandhousepublishing.com

**Fax orders to:** 866-496-3139 (fax this completed form)

**Postal orders to:** Sutherland House Publishing
P.O. Box 8683
Tucson, AZ, 85738

**Please send me _____ copies of *"It's a Crisis! Now What?"* The first step-by-step crisis communications guide for the global tourism and hospitality professional at $24.95 each, plus shipping and handling.**

Name: _____

Company:_____

Address: _____

City: _____ State: _____ Zip:_____

Area Code/Phone #: _____

Email address: _____

**Sales Tax:** Please add 6.6% for products shipped to Arizona addresses.

**Shipping**

**US and Canada:** $U.S. 4 for first book, $U.S. 2 each additional
**International:** $U.S. 9 for first book, $U.S. 5 each additional

**Payment type:** ☐ Check ☐ Credit card
☐ Visa ☐ Mastercard ☐ Discover

Credit Card #: _____

Name on card: _____ exp date: _____

**Please send more FREE information on:**

☐ Speaking/Seminars/Workshops ☐ Consulting ☐ Free webinars

**Please circle:** Public Relations Branding Crisis Communications

Sutherland House Publishing
Tucson, AZ 85738
SutherlandHousePublishing.com

# QUICK ORDER FORM

**Web orders to:**    www.sutherlandhousepublishing.com

**Email orders to:**    orders@sutherlandhousepublishing.com

**Fax orders to:**    866-496-3139 (fax this completed form)

**Postal orders to:**    Sutherland House Publishing
P.O. Box 8683
Tucson, AZ, 85738

**Please send me** _____ **copies of** *"It's a Crisis! Now What?"* **The first step-by-step crisis communications guide for the global tourism and hospitality professional at $24.95 each, plus shipping and handling.**

Name: _____

Company: _____

Address: _____

City: _____ State: _____ Zip: _____

Area Code/Phone #: _____

Email address: _____

**Sales Tax:** Please add 6.6% for products shipped to Arizona addresses.

**Shipping**

**US and Canada:** $U.S. 4 for first book, $U.S. 2 each additional
**International:** $U.S. 9 for first book, $U.S. 5 each additional

**Payment type:**   ☐ Check      ☐ Credit card
☐ Visa      ☐ Mastercard      ☐ Discover

Credit Card #: _____

Name on card: _____ exp date: _____

**Please send more FREE information on:**
☐ Speaking/Seminars/Workshops   ☐ Consulting   ☐ Free webinars

**Please circle:**  Public Relations    Branding    Crisis Communications